LESSONS OF LIFE TO ACHIEVE YOUR DREAMS

For Today's Youth

Steven N. Dial, Sr.

Orman Press
Lithonia, GA

ISBN 1-891773-19-4

Printed in the United States of America

Published by Orman Press Inc.
4200 Sandy Lake Drive
Lithonia, GA 30038
(770) 808-0999

LESSONS OF LIFE
TO ACHIEVE YOUR DREAMS
For Today's Youth

Steven N. Dial, Sr.

CONTENTS

Much love:

To my lovely wife, Robin, without whose help I could not have achieved my dream of writing this book and for standing beside me in all that the Lord allows me to do;

To my sons, Steven N. E. Dial, II and Micah K. Dial, for being strong, happy, and handsome "Daddy's boys;"

To my mother for always pushing me to be the best that I can be;

To my pastor, the Rev. Dr. George O. McCalep, Jr., for being my spiritual father, role model, and mentor;

To my neighbor for life, my friend, typesetter, and copy editor, Cassandra R. Baker, for your friendship and continuous help;

To Johnice McRae, who embraced my vision from the very start; may God bless you Floyd, Jabari, Jelani, and Jayla;

To attorney Laurene Sanders Duhart, for our power lunches that keep me inspired;

To Reta L. Bigham, for always being the "ram in the bush"—love 'ya;

To Ann Gilner, for always telling me the truth even when it hurts. You are a blessing;;

To Shirley Moore, for being faithful to Children Planting Seeds Family Daily Devotional, may God bless you Joe, Ayana, and Joseph;

To my brother in the ministry, the Rev. Maury Patton, for believing in me and encouraging me to keep going when things were tough, thanks for standing in the gap for me and my family;

To 23 nieces and nephews who have help prepare me for being a youth pastor and publisher of *Children Planting Seeds Family Daily Devotional*;

To the children and youth—past, present, and future—whose lives I have touched and will touch at Greenforest Community Baptist Church and those around the country who read these words.

HOW TO USE THIS BOOK

This book should be used to inspire a young person to dream, plan, and do something with their dreams and the plans they make. A dream is no good without a plan and a plan is no good if you can't write it down, and a plan is no good if you don't share it with someone who will encourage you to do something with it. This book is designed to help young people think and evaluate themselves. It is important for young people to start early with self evaluation. It is our desire to get young people to look within and bring out the gifts that God has placed inside of them.

This book should be used in the classroom and in Sunday School classes. Through oral recitation and my interactive web-site (www.StevenDial.com) and through e-mail (dreams@StevenDial.com), youth should be encouraged to discuss and expand upon such concepts as ATTITUDE, BEHAVIOR, COMMITMENT, DETERMINATION, PERSEVERANCE, as well as the development of a five year plan.

FROM THE AUTHOR

Life is a gift from God, a gift that is very precious. The lessons you learn in life are very important because they help you make the best out of life (gift) that God has given you. Dreams are wonderful because no one can tell you what to dream and what not to dream. There is no limit and dreams do come true. You've heard people say they bought their dream house or car and that's all good. But what about saying I have my dream life.

In this life, sometimes you are going to feel like you cannot make it, but I want you to know that you can and you will achieve your dreams. Great men and women don't become great by themselves; they become great because they have built their lives on great principles. It does not matter where you live or the color of your skin or how much money you have. Build your life on godly principles and you will be successful in life. It might take time, but you will achieve your dreams.

Throughout this book and my interactive web-site (www.StevenDial.com) I want to be your internet youth pastor, someone who will pray for you and help you develop the godly principles outlined in this book. I want to help you with your plans for life. Remember this saying, "People don't plan to fail, they fail to plan." Let's plan together.

— *SND*

FOREWORD

ADF;LKJ ADF;LKJADF ;LLKJASDF;L ADSFN;NAD;LKNK

ADF;LNADSF ;LASF ASDF;LKNASDF
ADSF;LKNASDF;L ;AL

AD;FLKNADF ASDF
ADF;LKNADSF

ATTITUDE

A calm and undisturbed mind and heart are the life and health of the body, but envy, jealousy, and wrath are like rottenness of the bones. —Proverbs 14:30

"A"

Attitude - a state of mind or manner of carrying oneself.

A is for Attitude. Not just any attitude, but a positive attitude. If you can keep a positive attitude, you will become whatever God wants you to be. Keep a positive attitude in all that you do. Remember that people always remember the type of attitude you had. You will soon see that when you have a positive attitude you tend to do a better job and enjoy the task more than if you do not demonstrate a good attitude.

❧ Plant This:

A positive attitude is everything.

Prayer: Hallelujah, thank you, God. I am so glad you have blessed me with a great attitude. Amen.

Your
attitude
overshadows
anything
that
you
do
or
say.
-S.N.D.

Write your ATTITUDE quote by which you live:

____

____

____

____

____

List three areas in your life
where you need a better attitude:

1. ____________________________

2. ____________________________

3. ____________________________

❧

List three areas in your life
where you have a great attitude:

1. ____________________________

2. ____________________________

3. ____________________________

When you've completed your ATTITUDE assignment, go to my web-site at www.stevendial.com for a 10-minute motivational message to help you improve your ATTITUDE.

E-mail me your ATTITUDE quote at dreams@stevendial.com.

BEHAVIOR

Even a child is know by his doings, whether his work be pure, and whether it be right. —Proverbs 20:11

"B"

Behavior - one's actions or reactions under specified circumstances.

B is for Behavior. Today, and every day, practice good behavior. Did you know that people will remember your behavior long after you are gone? Don't be left out of fun activities because someone doesn't trust your behavior. It has been said, "The things you do speak so loud that I can't hear a word you're saying." Start right now by showing others that you can be on your best behavior under any circumstance.

Plant This:

Be on your best behavior.

Prayer: Hallelujah, thank you, God. Dear Father, please bless me to always be on my best behavior. Amen.

A
well
behaved
person
reaps
many
of
the
good
benefits
of
life.
-SND

Write your behavior quote by which you live:

List three areas in your life
where you need to exhibit better behavior:

1. ______________________________

2. ______________________________

3. ______________________________

❧

List three areas in your life
where you exhibit good behavior:

1. ______________________________

2. ______________________________

3. ______________________________

When you've completed your BEHAVIOR assignment, go to my web-site at www.stevendial.com for a 10-minute motivational message to help you improve your BEHAVIOR.

E-mail me your BEHAVIOR quote at dreams@stevendial.com.

COMMITMENT

Commit thy way unto the Lord; trust also in him; and he shall bring it to pass. —Psalm 37:5

"C"

C is for Commitment. Try being committed to something. You will have the chance to do many things throughout your young life. Pick one important thing and be committed to completing it. Here are some examples of things you can commit to over the next few months:

1) Commit to reading at least 10 books this year.

2) Work on an art project that will require your commitment and devotion.

3) Commit to visiting an elderly person once a week this year.

Whatever you commit to do this year, do it well and God will bless you.

Plant This:

Be committed!

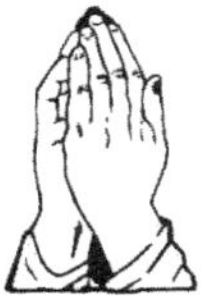

Prayer: Hallelujah, thank you, God. Dear God, continue to teach me the importance of commitment. Amen.

Commitment
teaches
you
to
understand
the
situation
better
than
anyone
else.
-SND

Write your commitment quote by which you live:

List three areas in your life
where you need to be more committed:

1. ____________________________

2. ____________________________

3. ____________________________

❧

List three areas in your life
where you are committed:

1. ____________________________

2. ____________________________

3. ____________________________

When you've completed your COMMITMENT assignment, go to my web-site at www.stevendial.com for a 10-minute motivational message to help you improve your COMMITMENT.

E-mail me your COMMITMENT quote at dreams@stevendial.com.

---

www.stevendial.com

DETERMINATION

Fight the good fight of faith, lay hold on eternal life, where unto thou art also called, and hast professed a good profession before many witnesses. —1 Timothy 6:12

"D"

Determination - to stand firm in a purpose.

D is for Determination. Always be determined to see things through. You have to be determined to achieve your goals. Ask God to grant you the spirit of determination. Don't be afraid to show determination in all that you do. Once you begin to demonstrate determination, you will see that God will continue to give you the knowledge that you need to do well in life and in school. When you are determined to succeed you will always achieve your goals. Determination is one of the key ingredients to excelling in school and in life. God loves it when you are determined to do well.

❧ Plant This:

Be determined to follow Jesus.

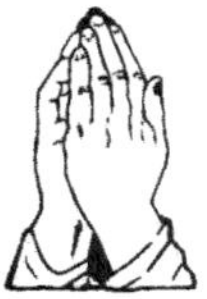

Prayer: Hallelujah, thank you, God. I ask you today, dear God, to give me the spirit of determination. Amen.

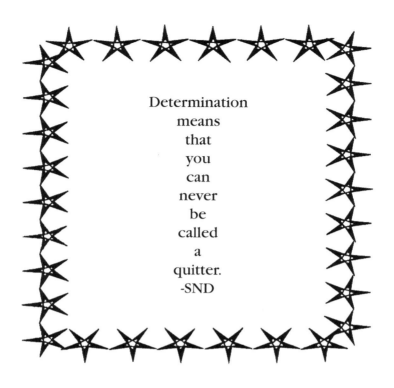

Determination
means
that
you
can
never
be
called
a
quitter.
-SND

Write your determination quote by which you live:

____

____

____

____

____

List three areas in your life
where you need to be more determined:

1. ____________________________

2. ____________________________

3. ____________________________

❧

List three areas in your life
where you have determination:

1. ____________________________

2. ____________________________

3. ____________________________

When you've completed your DETERMINATION assignment, go to my web-site at www.stevendial.com for a 10-minute motivational message to help you improve your DETERMINATION.

E-mail me your DETERMINATION quote at dreams@stevendial.com.

EXCELLENCE

O Lord our Lord, how excellent is thy name in all the earth.
—Psalm 8:1

"E"

Excellence - superiority or exceptionally good.

E is for Excellence. When you are being determined and committed to different tasks, make sure that you are doing an excellent job. God always wants your very best. God wants you to be exceptional in all that you do. When you look back on all the great things that you have done, you will be most pleased with those things that turned out excellent. For instance, when you receive an "A" on your assignment or someone gives you excellent remarks of on job done well, it makes you feel great. Never settle for less than your very best. Don't forget that it always feels good when you have done an excellent job.

❧ Plant This:

How excellent is God's name!

Prayer: Hallelujah, thank you, God. Dear God, please help me to strive for excellence in everything I do. Amen.

I
have learned
that
by doing
something
right
the
first
time
you
will never
have
to
do it
over again.
-SND

Write your quote of excellence by which you live:

____

____

____

____

____

List three areas in your life
where you need to show excellence:

1. ____________________________

2. ____________________________

3. ____________________________

❧

List three areas in your life
where you are showing excellence:

1. ____________________________

2. ____________________________

3. ____________________________

When you've completed your EXCELLENCE assignment, go to my web-site at www.stevendial.com for a 10-minute motivational message to help you improve your EXCELLENCE.

E-mail me your EXCELLENCE quote at dreams@stevendial.com.

FAITH

But without faith it is impossible to please God.
—Hebrews 11:6

"F"

Faith - belief not based on logical proof.

F is for Faith. If you but have a tiny bit of faith, God will do the rest. If you are ever afraid or unsure of something, you can always rely on your faith in God. God understands our fears and he wants us to have faith in Him. It is sometimes hard to rely or turn to your faith because it seems unbelievable that anything can be done to help you out. But God said in His word that all we need is faith the size of a mustard seed—and that's not much at all. Most young people think that only older people use faith. Do not fall into that category of people. It is important that you know and understand that your faith is the only thing that will see you through all of life's circumstances. Do not wait. Start living by faith today.

Plant This:

Where is your faith?

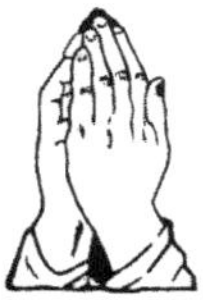

Prayer: Hallelujah, thank you, God. Dear God, please help me to become full of faith. Amen.

God
has
made
faith
so available
to
us
that
we should
use it
as
often
as
we can.
-SND

Write your quote of faith by which you live:

List three areas in your life where you need more faith:

1. ______________________________

2. ______________________________

3. ______________________________

List three areas in your life where you have good faith:

1. ______________________________

2. ______________________________

3. ______________________________

When you've completed your FAITH assignment, go to my web-site at www.stevendial.com for a 10-minute motivational message to help you improve your FAITH.

E-mail me your FAITH quote at dreams@stevendial.com.

GOODNESS

He loveth righteousness and judgment; the earth is full of the goodness of the Lord. —Psalm 33:5

"G"

G is for Goodness. Most of us have heard people say that God is good! Take a moment to think of just how good God has already been to **you**. Today, make a list of things God has given you, and then make another list of things that others may not have. Compare the two lists. God is good! Isn't he? God's goodness is so overwhelming and he continues to bless each of us uniquely. Always thank God for being so good to you. As young people, we sometimes only think of the many things that we want, but today start thinking of what you already have and be grateful for God's goodness.

❧ Plant This:

Isn't God good?

Prayer: Hallelujah, thank you, God. God I just want to say "Thank you" for being so good to me. Amen.

God
is
good
all
the
time;
we
should
try
to
be
good
most
of
the
time.
-SND

Write your quote of goodness by which you live:

____

____

____

____

____

List three areas in your life where you need a better attitude towards realizing God's goodness:

1. ______________________

2. ______________________

3. ______________________

❧

List three areas in your life where you have a great attitude towards realizing God's goodness:

1. ______________________

2. ______________________

3. ______________________

When you've completed your GOODNESS assignment, go to my web-site at www.stevendial.com for a 10-minute motivational message to help you improve your GOODNESS.

E-mail me your GOODNESS quote at dreams@stevendial.com.

HARD WORK

But let every man prove his own work, and then shall he have rejoicing in himself alone and not in another.
—Galatians 6:4

"H"

Hard work - stern or strict work.

H is for Hard Work. Don't say, "Oh, boy," and don't turn the page! Many young people try hard to avoid a little hard work. Many young people do not believe that they should do any hard work. God wants us to be able to handle hard work from time to time. God wants you to be able to appreciate the not so hard times. Hard work in school pays off with good grades. Hard work for Jesus gets us to heaven. If you learn to put forth the effort to work hard today, as you become older you'll find that you won't have to work as hard. God blesses hard work and he also rewards us for it.

❧ Plant This:

Don't be afraid of a little hard work.

Prayer: Hallelujah, thank you, God. As I grow, help me to appreciate hard work. Amen.

Hard
work
today
makes
for
little
work
tomorrow.
-SND

Write your quote of hard work by which you live:

____

____

____

____

____

List three areas in your life where you need a better attitude towards hard work:

1. ______________________________

2. ______________________________

3. ______________________________

❧

List three areas in your life where you have a great attitude towards hard work:

1. ______________________________

2. ______________________________

3. ______________________________

When you've completed your HARD WORK assignment, go to my web-site at www.stevendial.com for a 10-minute motivational message to help you improve your HARD WORK.

E-mail me your HARD WORK quote at dreams@stevendial.com.

INTELLIGENCE

The heart of the prudent getteth knowledge; and the ear of the wise seeketh knowledge. —Proverbs 18:15

"I"

Intelligence - the ability to apply knowledge.

I is for Intelligence. Are you intelligent? Do you like being around intelligent people? God loves intelligent children. God wants us all to be intelligent. Adults are pleased when young people have intelligent behavior. You and your friends will be in many situations where you will be able to choose whether to act intelligently or unintelligently. Since you represent Jesus, which will you choose—intelligent or unintelligent? The choice is yours. Intelligent decisions always work out for your good. When you stop and think things through, the intelligent choice becomes clearer to you. Don't always rush through things. Take your time and make intelligent choices.

❧ Plant This:

Intelligent people achieve great things.

Prayer: Hallelujah, thank you, God. It is my prayer that I act intelligently at all times. Amen.

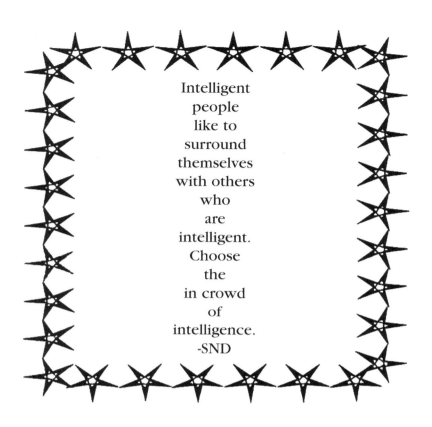

Intelligent
people
like to
surround
themselves
with others
who
are
intelligent.
Choose
the
in crowd
of
intelligence.
-SND

Write your quote of intelligence by which you live:

List three areas in your life where you need to demonstrate intelligence:

1. ____________________________

2. ____________________________

3. ____________________________

❧

List three areas in your life where you demonstrate great intelligence:

1. ____________________________

2. ____________________________

3. ____________________________

When you've completed your INTELLIGENCE assignment, go to my web-site at www.stevendial.com for a 10-minute motivational message to help you improve your INTELLIGENCE.

E-mail me your INTELLIGENCE quote at dreams@stevendial.com.

JOY

My brethren, count it all joy when ye fall into divers temptations. —James 1:2

"J"

Joy - great pleasure or happiness.

J is for Joy. Have you ever heard an adult say, "Joy comes in the morning?" Have you ever wondered what that meant? Sometimes things don't always go well and you may think that they won't get better. But if you keep the *faith*, continue to do *hard work*, have a positive *attitude*, be *committed*, be *determined*—always do an excellent job and be on your best *behavior*, God will allow the sun to shine for you. Having the spirit of joy gives you a peace that surpasses all understanding. People who possess a true spirit of joy bring joy to everyone they meet. Joy is not something that you can pretend to have. Either you have it or you don't.

Plant This:

Joy to the world!

Prayer: Hallelujah, thank you, God. Please God, fill my heart with joy. Amen.

You
can't
fake
joy.
It's
as
natural
as
breathing.
-SND

Write your quote of joy by which you live:

List three areas in your life where you need to portray more joy:

1. ______________________________

2. ______________________________

3. ______________________________

❧

List three areas in your life where you portray great joy:

1. ______________________________

2. ______________________________

3. ______________________________

When you've completed your JOY assignment, go to my web-site at www.stevendial.com for a 10-minute motivational message to help you improve your JOY.

E-mail me your JOY quote at dreams@stevendial.com.

KINDNESS

...but with everlasting kindness will I have mercy on thee, saith the Lord thy redeemer. —Isaiah 54:8

"K"

Kindness - pleasant and kind nature.

K is for Kindness. Being kind to others certainly pleases God. Sometimes if you know that someone needs a little cheering up, try saying a kind word or doing a kind deed for that person. If you want God to smiles down on you, start today by helping someone who is in need. Make a list of the kind things that you can do to help someone who is in need. Sometimes when you have hard time being kind to others, think of just how kind God is to you. God doesn't even hold grudges when we forget to be kind to him. Kindness is a characteristic that can't be beat.

❧ Plant This:

A kind deed is worth a thousand words.

Prayer: Hallelujah, thank you, God. Teach me to be kind to others. Amen.

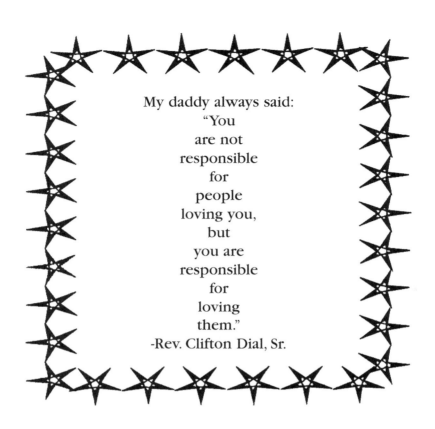

My daddy always said:
"You
are not
responsible
for
people
loving you,
but
you are
responsible
for
loving
them."
-Rev. Clifton Dial, Sr.

Write your quote of kindness by which you live:

____

____

____

____

____

List three areas in your life where you need to work on being kind:

1. ______________________________

2. ______________________________

3. ______________________________

❧

List three areas in your life where you show kindness:

1. ______________________________

2. ______________________________

3. ______________________________

When you've completed your KINDNESS assignment, go to my web-site at www.stevendial.com for a 10-minute motivational message to help you improve your KINDNESS.

E-mail me your KINDNESS quote at dreams@stevendial.com.

LOYALTY

Trust in the Lord with all thine heart; and lean not unto thine own understanding. —Proverbs 3:5

"L"

Loyalty - devoted attachment or allegiance to a person or thing.

L is for Loyalty. When you are loyal to someone, you will stand by him or her not matter what. Regardless of what other people decide to do, you will remain loyal to the cause. Don't you think it would please God if we have this type of loyalty to Him? Learn to be loyal to God and to things that would please God. Being loyal is a characteristic that God and others will admire. When God sees that you are loyal to a good cause, he will bless that loyalty. As you continue to make new friends and new decisions, be sure that your loyalty remains in the right place.

❧ Plant This:

Loyalty goes a long way.

Prayer: Hallelujah, thank you, God. Dear God, teach me the importance of loyalty. Amen.

Believe
in
loyalty.
Expect
loyalty.
Be
loyal.
-SND

Write your quote of loyalty by which you live:

List three areas in your life where you need a greater amount of loyalty:

1. ______________________________

2. ______________________________

3. ______________________________

❧

List three areas in your life where you need a greater amount of loyalty:

1. ______________________________

2. ______________________________

3. ______________________________

When you've completed your LOYALTY assignment, go to my web-site at www.stevendial.com for a 10-minute motivational message to help you improve your LOYALTY.

E-mail me your LOYALTY quote at dreams@stevendial.com.

MOTIVATION

My son, attend unto my wisdom, and bow thine ear to my understanding. —Proverbs 5:1

"M"

Motivation - an incentive to impel.

M is for Motivation. Have you ever needed to push to get something done? Did you ever need someone to say a few encouraging words to help you to do what needed to be done? Well, what you needed was motivation. It is also a blessing to motivate others when they need it. There are many ways you can be motivated. You may need to read motivational books or listen to motivational speakers. But always remember that the best motivational speaker is God and the best motivational book is the *Bible*. Sometimes things may not always go your way, but if you stay motivated it will be easy to stay on track. Being motivated is one of the very first requirements of doing something well. So, get motivated and remain motivated.

❧ Plant This:

Stay motivated.

Prayer: Hallelujah, thank you, God. Dear God, continue to help me to be motivated in all that I do. Amen.

Sometimes
the
best
motivator
you
can
have
is
yourself.
Remember
God + you
make
a
majority.
-SND

Write your quote of motivation by which you live:

____

____

____

____

____

List three areas in your life where you need to work on your level of motivation:

1. ____________________________

2. ____________________________

3. ____________________________

❧

List three areas in your life where you have a great level of motivation:

1. ____________________________

2. ____________________________

3. ____________________________

When you've completed your MOTIVATION assignment, go to my web-site at www.stevendial.com for a 10-minute motivational message to help you improve your MOTIVATION.

E-mail me your MOTIVATION quote at dreams@stevendial.com.

NOBLENESS

Keep thy heart with all diligence; for out of it are the issues of life. —Proverbs 4:23

"N"

Nobleness - displaying high moral character.

N is for Nobleness. Being noble can sometimes be hard for both adults and children. Oftentimes being noble can be mistaken for being nerdy or wimpy. This is not true. Being noble to others who deserve it builds character in you. Being noble also encourages others to have respect for you. God blesses nobility with great moral character. Nobility makes it easy for others to trust you and when people trust you, they allow you to do certain privileged things. Being noble will also make you feel good about yourself.

Plant This:

A noble person is a wise person.

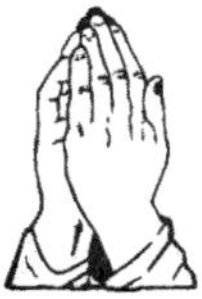

Prayer: Hallelujah, thank you, God. God give me the strength to be a noble child of God. Amen.

My
dad
was
a
noble
man.
He
always
said,
"People
have to
see
God
in you,
Stevie."
-SND

Write your quote of nobleness by which you live:

List three areas in your life where you need to work on being noble:

1. ____________________________

2. ____________________________

3. ____________________________

❧

List three areas in your life where you have a great amount of nobleness:

1. ____________________________

2. ____________________________

3. ____________________________

When you've completed your NOBLENESS assignment, go to my web-site at www.stevendial.com for a 10-minute motivational message to help you improve your NOBLENESS.

E-mail me your NOBLENESS quote at dreams@stevendial.com.

www.stevendial.com

OPTIMISM

The glory of young men is their strength: and the beauty of old me is the grey head. —Proverbs 20:29

"O"

Optimistic - to expect a favorable or good outcome.

O is for Optimistic. "It is not that bad." "Look on the bright side." These are all things that an optimistic person would probably say. Imagine a glass of water that is half full. Is it half full or half empty? Someone said that it depends on how thirsty you are. God wants you to believe that the glass if half full or the situation is not that bad. The next time something is not going well, be optimistic. Have faith in God and watch Him work it out. When you have a negative attitude about something, you have already allowed that situation to get the best of you. When you remain optimistic, you always leave room for that miracle to happen.

Plant This:

God will show up and show out.

Prayer: Hallelujah, thank you, God. Being optimistic is a characteristic I want you to bless me with. Amen.

It
takes
the
same
amount
of energy
to expect
a miracle
as it
takes to
expect
a disaster.
Take
your pick.
-SND

Write your quote of optimism by which you live:

____

____

____

____

____

List three areas in your life where you need to be more optimistic:

1. ______________________________

2. ______________________________

3. ______________________________

❧

List three areas in your life about which you are optimistic:

1. ______________________________

2. ______________________________

3. ______________________________

When you've completed your OPTIMISM assignment, go to my web-site at www.stevendial.com for a 10-minute motivational message to help you improve your OPTIMISM.

E-mail me your OPTIMISM quote at dreams@stevendial.com.

POWER

Where the word of a king is, there is power.
—Ecclesiastes 8:4

"P"

Power - to have authority or control.

P is for Power. Did you know that you have the power to move mountains? Well, yes you do. Deep down inside of each one of us is a certain amount of power. God gave each of us enough to fight off evil things that may come our way. The next time that you think you can't, just say, "Yes I can. God gave me the power." Remember that God has all power in the palm of His hand. When you open your hand and place it in God's hand, he passes the power to you to achieve your dreams. Remember that the power of God is always inside of you waiting to come out.

❧ Plant This:

I've got the power!

Prayer: Hallelujah, thank you, God. Teach me to use the power that you have given me to do great things. Amen.

The
most
powerful
man
in
the
world
lives
inside
of
me—
don't
mess
with
me!
-SND

Write your quote of power by which you live:

List three areas in your life where you are not displaying power:

1. ____________________________

2. ____________________________

3. ____________________________

❧

List three areas in your life where you are displaying power:

1. ____________________________

2. ____________________________

3. ____________________________

When you've completed your POWER assignment, go to my web-site at www.stevendial.com for a 10-minute motivational message to help you improve your POWER.

E-mail me your POWER quote at dreams@stevendial.com.

QUICKEN

...quicken thou me according to thy word. —Psalm 119:25

"Q"

Quicken - to make or bring alive: to vitalize or stimulate.

Q is for Quicken. God's word and His deeds should make your heart quicken. Every time you think of God and all that He has done, you should feel alive and stimulated. God's love for you should make you feel good inside. The word quicken is a funny sounding word that should make you feel all funny inside. When you think of achieving your dreams you should fee a quickening inside of you. God wants you to be vitalized and stimulated when doing great things.

❧ Plant This:

My heart quickens for God.

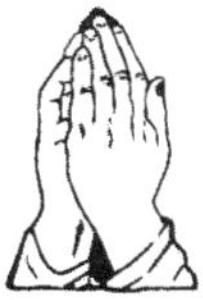

Prayer: Hallelujah, thank you, God. Thank you for allowing me to learn new and exciting things about your word everyday. Amen.

When
God
is
your
source
you
will
always
find
yourself
quickened
in
the
spirit.
-SND

Write your quote of quickenness by which you live:

____

____

____

____

____

List three areas in your life where you need to practice your quickening skills:

1. ______________________

2. ______________________

3. ______________________

❧

List three areas in your life where you are utilizing your quickening skills:

1. ______________________

2. ______________________

3. ______________________

When you've completed your QUICKEN assignment, go to my web-site at www.stevendial.com for a 10-minute motivational message to help you improve your ability to QUICKEN the spirit.

E-mail me your QUICKEN quote at dreams@stevendial.com

RELIGION

If any man among you seem to be religious, and bridleth not his tongue, but deceiveth his own heart, this man's religion is vain. —James 1:26

"R"

Religion - belief and reverence for a supernatural power accepted as the creator of the universe.

R is for Religion. Religion is a word that means so many different things to so many different people. Always think of your religion as holy and sacred. Remember to always stand firm in your belief in Jesus Christ and your Father, God the Creator. Be committed to learn as much as you can about your religion. Allow your religious views to be the backbone of all that you do. Allow your religion and beliefs to be your solid foundation. With a solid foundation you can only go up.

❧ Plant This:

I've got good religion.

Prayer: Hallelujah, thank you, God. I'm so glad I've got religion. Thank you, Lord. Amen.

Religion
is
good,
but
don't
get
hung
up on
the
word.
Get
hung up
on
JESUS.
-SND

Write your quote of religion by which you live:

____

____

____

____

____

List three areas in your life where you need a better attitude towards religion:

1. ____________________________

2. ____________________________

3. ____________________________

❧

List three areas in your life where you have a great attitude towards religion:

1. ____________________________

2. ____________________________

3. ____________________________

When you've completed your RELIGION assignment, go to my web-site at www.stevendial.com for a 10-minute motivational message to help you improve your RELIGION.

E-mail me your RELIGION quote at dreams@stevendial.com.

SURRENDER

And he said to them all, if any man will come after me, let him deny himself, and take up his cross daily, and follow me. —Luke 9:23

"S"

Surrender - to give up or abandon.

S is for Surrender. God is a jealous God. God wants you to surrender your all to him. Turn your entire life over to God and watch how exciting your life will become. God wants your time, talent, your fears, and your dreams. When you have truly surrendered your entire life to God, then and only then will He know that you love Him with all your heart. If there are any bad habits that you have that may be slowing you down or causing you to miss out on your dreams, surrender them over to Jesus. Remember that this is God's fight, not yours. Surrender is all to him.

❧ Plant This:

I surrender all.

Prayer: Hallelujah, thank you, God. Even though I am young, teach me to surrender my entire life to you. Amen.

When
you
give
up
something
for
God,
He
will
give
something
to
you.
-SND

Write your quote of surrender by which you live:

List three areas in your life where you need a better spirit towards surrendering:

1. ______________________________

2. ______________________________

3. ______________________________

❧

List three areas in your life where you have a great spirit of surrendering:

1. ______________________________

2. ______________________________

3. ______________________________

When you've completed your SURRENDER assignment, go to my web-site at www.stevendial.com for a 10-minute motivational message to help you improve your ability to SURRENDER.

E-mail me your SURRENDER quote at dreams@stevendial.com.

TEMPTATION

Then Peter said unto her, How is it that ye have agreed together to tempt the Spirit of the Lord? —Acts 5:9

"T"

Temptation - enticement or inducement.

T is for Temptation. Sometimes things look good and inviting, but does that make it good for you? Temptation will be all around you always. Most of the time it is pretty easy to make the right decision but at others times it's not easy. Ask God to help you to make the right decision. God doesn't want to trick you; he is not in the tricking business, just the blessing business. Remember God wants you to be blessed. The devil wants you to yield to many temptations but because you are deeply rooted in God and in your achievements for the future, you will not yield to those temptations. Do not be fooled. Be smart.

❧ Plant This:

Don't yield to temptation.

Prayer: Hallelujah, thank you, God. Sometimes I am tempted to do the wrong thing. Help me to make the right decision. Amen.

It might
look good,
sound good,
feel good,
or even
smell good,
but
that
doesn't mean
it's
good
for
you.
-SND

Write your quote of temptation by which you live:

____

____

____

____

____

List three areas in your life where you need to work on temptation:

1. ______________________

2. ______________________

3. ______________________

❧

List three areas in your life where you have mastered a temptation:

1. ______________________

2. ______________________

3. ______________________

When you've completed your TEMPTATION assignment, go to my web-site at www.stevendial.com for a 10-minute motivational message to help you improve your ability to not to yield to TEMPTATION.

E-mail me your TEMPTATION quote at dreams@stevendial.com.

UPRIGHT

The integrity of the upright shall guide them.
—Proverbs 11:3

"U"

Upright - to be honest.

U is for Upright. If you can learn to live upright you will be a person that others can learn to trust. An upright person is an honest person. God blesses his children who live upright. We all have heard that honesty is the best policy. Well, we also know that honesty is God's policy. Honor God by living an upright life for Him. What things can you do in order to live an upright life? What things can you do to be a honest person? When you fail to be an upright person, your dreams will begin to crumble and you may not know why. It's not old-fashioned to be upright. It's in fashion.

Plant This:

Upright people do not just exist in the *Bible*.

Prayer: Hallelujah, thank you, God. I want to be an upright child of God. Amen.

Live
right.
Live
long.
-SND

Write your quote of being upright by which you live:

List three areas in your life where you need to practice living upright:

1. ______________________

2. ______________________

3. ______________________

❧

List three areas in your life where you have a great attitude towards leading an upright life:

1. ______________________

2. ______________________

3. ______________________

When you've completed your UPRIGHT assignment, go to my web-site at www.stevendial.com for a 10-minute motivational message to help you improve your ability to be UPRIGHT.

E-mail me your UPRIGHT quote at dreams@stevendial.com.

VIGOR

I can do all things through Christ which strengtheneth me.
—Philippians 4:13

"V"

Vigor - having energy or physical strength.

V is for Vigor. Do you love to play and are you always ready to do something fun? You are probably full of vigor. Start today by using some of your energy to work for Jesus. Be vigorous in your studies and in your love for God. Do not waste energy on negative things. Save all of your energy to help build God's kingdom. God has given young people more energy so that they can vigorously work for Him. Always utilize your energy for good. Don't forget that temptation is always trying to win your soul, but the well-equipped saint with vigor and zeal will always win.

❧ Plant This:

Be full of vigor for God.

Prayer: Hallelujah, thank you, God. Help me to turn all of my vigor into good use for God. Amen.

I
work
out
with
Jesus
each
day.
Thus,
I
am
always
physically
and
spiritually
fit.
-SND

Write your quote of being vigorous by which you live:

List three areas in your life where you need to exercise the amount of vigor in your life:

1. ______________________________

2. ______________________________

3. ______________________________

❧

List three areas in your life where you utilize lots of vigor in your life:

1. ______________________________

2. ______________________________

3. ______________________________

When you've completed your VIGOR assignment, go to my web-site at www.stevendial.com for a 10-minute motivational message to help you improve your ability to be full of VIGOR.

E-mail me your VIGOR quote at dreams@stevendial.com.

WISDOM

He that getteth wisdom loveth his own soul: he that keepeth understanding shall find good. —Proverbs 19:8

"W"

Wisdom - ability to understand what is right; having good judgment.

W is for Wisdom. A wise child is a smart child. Smart children of God use good judgment when they are making decisions. God wants you to have wisdom and understanding. It is easy to be a part of the not-so-wise crowd, but it takes great effort and smarts to become a wise child of God. As you continue to grow in God's love, practice the art of being wise. The one who makes the wisest choices are the ones who please God. Wisdom is a gift from God. He wants you to be a wise steward over all that he has given you. Wise children of God lead rewarding and fulfilling lives.

Plant This:

Wisdom is wonderful!

Prayer: Hallelujah, thank you, God. O God, I pray that you will give me wisdom as I grow in your love. Amen.

Street
smarts
and
common
sense
are
okay,
but
give
me
wisdom;
it
comes
from
God.
-SND

Write your quote of wisdom by which you live:

____

____

____

____

____

List three areas in your life where you need wisdom:

1. ______________________________

2. ______________________________

3. ______________________________

❧

List three areas in your life where you have wisdom:

1. ______________________________

2. ______________________________

3. ______________________________

When you've completed your WISDOM assignment, go to my web-site at www.stevendial.com for a 10-minute motivational message to help you improve your ability to have WISDOM.

E-mail me your WISDOM quote at dreams@stevendial.com.

www.stevendial.com

XYLOPHONE

Praise the Lord with harp: sing unto him with the psaltery and an instrument of ten strings. —Psalm 33:2

"X"

Xylophone - a musical instrument made of wooden bars of different sizes.

Have you ever listened to someone play a xylophone? Well, it has a beautiful sound. You don't see xylophones as much as you see other instruments like trumpets or drums. Did you know that Jesus enjoys the sound of music? Jesus wants us to make a joyful noise unto Him. I hope that you will have a chance to play a xylophone because I'm sure you will love the melodious sound. Always use your musical gifts or talents to the glory of God. When you do, know that God is smiling down on you. It should make you feel good to know that you made God smile.

❧ Plant This:

Jesus loves sweet music.

Prayer: Hallelujah, thank you, God. Dear Lord, thank you for allowing me to praise you with instruments and songs. Amen.

Making
noise
is
only
important
when
you
are
praising
God.
-SND

Write your quote of praise by which you live:

List three areas in your life where you can exhibit praise to God:

1. ____________________________

2. ____________________________

3. ____________________________

List three areas in your life where you already exhibit praise to God:

1. ____________________________

2. ____________________________

3. ____________________________

When you've completed your XYLOPHONE (PRAISE) assignment, go to my web-site at www.stevendial.com for a 10-minute motivational message to help you improve your PRAISE.

E-mail me your PRAISE quote at dreams@stevendial.com.

YIELD

...but yield yourselves unto God, as those that are alive from the dead, and your members as instruments of righteousness unto God. —Romans 6:13

"Y"

Yield - to surrender.

Y is for Yield. We have always been taught that yield means to slow down. Well, God doesn't want you to slow down for certain things. God wants you to keep right on moving when you are faced with bad things such as fighting, cheating, stealing, using bad language, and any other thing that is ungodly. Remember to keep your mind on things that God likes. God will help you to avoid the bad things that come your way. If you've found yourself living too fast and making the wrong choices in life, then God, by all means, wants you to yield and slow down before it's too late. If you have made some really bad choices, God wants you to do more than yield. He wants you to stop!

❧ Plant This:

Yield not to temptation.

Prayer: Hallelujah, thank you, God. Dear Lord, continue to teach me not to yield to things that are not good for me. Amen.

Slow
your
roll.
If
you're
going
too
fast
you
might
miss
God.
-SND

Write your quote of yielding by which you live:

List three areas in your life where you need to slow down or yield:

1. ______________________

2. ______________________

3. ______________________

❧

List three areas in your life where you have learned to yield to something:

1. ______________________

2. ______________________

3. ______________________

When you've completed your YIELD assignment, go to my web-site at www.stevendial.com for a 10-minute motivational message to help you improve your YIELD.

E-mail me your YIELD quote at dreams@stevendial.com.

ZEAL

For I bear them record that they have a zeal for God, but not according to knowledge. —Romans 10:2

"Z"

Zeal - strong, eager feeling; enthusiasm.

Z is for Zeal. What excites you? What makes you really happy? Are you excited about life or school? If you are very excited and enthusiastic you are full of zeal. You should be full of zeal when it comes to God's word. When you are full of zeal, you have a passion for whatever you are excited about. Jesus wants us to have a passion for learning more about him. Jesus needs you to be full of zeal when you are helping to build God's kingdom. If you are excited about God's word the people who are around you will be excited, too. Continue to have a zeal for life and for your achievements. Continue to be eager to reach your goals and desires. Continue to be enthusiastic about all of the blessings that God has in store for you.

❧ Plant This:

Be zealous for the Lord!

Prayer: Hallelujah, thank you, God. I want to be excited and full of zeal when I study your word. Amen.

Live
life
with
a
purpose.
-SND

Write your quote of zeal by which you live:

List three areas in your life where you have an abundance of zeal:

1. ______________________

2. ______________________

3. ______________________

❧

List three areas in your life where you need to work on your amount of zeal:

1. ______________________

2. ______________________

3. ______________________

When you've completed your ZEAL assignment, go to my web-site at www.stevendial.com for a 10-minute motivational message to help you improve your ZEAL.

E-mail me your ZEAL quote at dreams@stevendial.com.

www.stevendial.com

THE FIVE-YEAR PLAN

What is a five-year plan? It is a life map to get you from one place in life to another. You may ask why do I need to write down my plan? If you don't write it down you might forget what your plans are. The reason why I suggest a five-year plan is so you won't be rushed. In having a five-year plan you will learn the value of patience. It is a virtue, a blessing. Patience brings great rewards; without it, great pain. The plan on the next pages is an example of a 13-year old who wants to become a lawyer.

Here are some steps in developing a five-year plan:

1. Pray to God for His direction.
2. Write down three things you would like to be doing five years from now.
3. Research, get some facts about whatever it is you want to be doing.
4. Find a mentor, someone who is doing what you want to be doing.
5. Write down your plans year by year.

Five-Year Plan
Age 13 - Year One (Lawyer)

❧ Commit your plan to God daily.

❧ Get a library card if you don't already have one.

❧ Ask yourself this question: What kind of lawyer do I want to become?

❧ Take two months and read about the different types of lawyers.

❧ Take the next three months to read about the three types of lawyers which you like best.

❧ For the next three months, locate three lawyers in the fields that you like best.

❧ During the next month, make an appointment with each one of the lawyers.

❧ Take the next three months to visit each of the lawyers. During your appointment, share your five-year plan, ask for input, ask if you may accompany them to court. Also ask if they would be your mentor for the next four years of your plan.

❧ Don't be discouraged if all of them don't agree.

❧ Trust in God. Remember that we put Him first in this plan; therefore, it's going to work.

Write your first-year plan:

When you've completed your ONE-YEAR PLAN assignment, go to my web-site at www.stevendial.com for a 10-minute motivational message to help you work on your ONE-YEAR PLAN.

E-mail me your ONE-YEAR PLAN quote at dreams@stevendial.com.

Five-Year Plan
Age 14 - Year Two (Lawyer)

- Commit your plan to God daily.
- Set up three appointments for the year with each mentor (lawyer).
- Ask each mentor to help you set up an appointment with a judge.
- Find out in which subjects you should excel.
- Subscribe to a law magazine.
- Let your school guidance counselor know about your plans.
- During the summer, attend an SAT/ACT seminar.
- Find three other persons around your age that also have a plan for the future. (Wait until after your first year before looking for other persons, because if you wait on others to get started you won't start.)

Write your second-year plan:

When you've completed your SECOND-YEAR PLAN assignment, go to my web-site at www.stevendial.com for a 10-minute motivational message to help you work on your SECOND-YEAR PLAN.

E-mail me your SECOND-YEAR PLAN quote at dreams@stevendial.com.

Five-Year Plan
Age 15 - Year Three (Lawyer)

- Commit your plan to God daily.

- Set up three appointments for the year with each mentor (lawyer).

- Set up three visits to a court case with each mentor (lawyer).

- Set up an appointment with a judge.

- Renew your magazine subscription.

- Get one of your mentors to allow you to volunteer to work in their office. Yes, I said "volunteer." Your payment will be knowledge.

- Ask your mentors and school guidance counselor to recommend colleges that have good law schools.

- Take SAT/ACT Test.

- Continue your SAT/ACT preparation.

- Work on your verbal skills.

- Choose three schools from your list and send for information.

- Visit the schools.

Write your third-year plan:

When you've completed your THIRD-YEAR PLAN assignment, go to my web-site at www.stevendial.com for a 10-minute motivational message to help you work on your THIRD-YEAR PLAN.

E-mail me your THIRD-YEAR PLAN quote at dreams@stevendial.com.

Five-Year Plan
Age 16 - Year Four (Lawyer)

- Commit your plan to God daily.

- Set up three appointments for the year with each mentor (lawyer). Ask questions.

- Renew your magazine subscription.

- Apply for admission at the three colleges you like best.

- Volunteer to work at one of your mentor's (lawyer's) office.

- Attend three different court cases this year.

- Communicate regularly with your school guidance counselor.

- Visit the schools. Ask questions.

Write your fourth-year plan:

When you've completed your FOURTH-YEAR PLAN assignment, go to my web-site at www.stevendial.com for a 10-minute motivational message to help you work on your FOURTH -YEAR PLAN.

E-mail me your FOURTH -YEAR PLAN quote at dreams@stevendial.com.

Five-Year Plan
Age 17 - Year Five (Lawyer)

❧ Commit your plan to God daily.

❧ Set up appointments for the year with each mentor (lawyer).

❧ Renew your magazine subscription.

❧ You, along with your family, should spend four days at the college where you have been accepted (Thursday, Friday, Saturday, Sunday).

❧ Find a freshman, sophomore, junior, senior, and a graduating senior who are majoring in law (mentors).

❧ Find other students who have a strong faith in God.

❧ Find a church to attend while you are in college.

You are now prepared knowledgeably and excited about what lies ahead—push forward.

Write your fifth-year plan:

Now that you have completed all the assignments, go to my web-site at www.stevendial.com and register for a thirty-minute consultation to discuss any issue of your life in which you would like my assistance.

See you on-line.

E-mail me your FIVE-YEAR PLAN quote at dreams@stevendial.com.

NOTES

LEARN TO FORGIVE

1. Write on a sheet of paper the names of the persons who have hurt you.

2. Face the hurt and the hate. It might be tough, but you will make it.

3. Realize that Jesus took upon Himself all the sins of the world. He made forgiveness possible.

4. Decide to forgive. When you decide not to forgive, you are telling God and others not to forgive you.

5. Take your list to God in prayer.

6. Destroy the list.

7. Pray daily for God to give you strength to never look back.

Never hold
grudges in life.
Grudges are
dream killers.
When you
hold a grudge,
in reality
the grudge
is holding
you.
-SND

THE SECRETS TO SUCCESS IN SCHOOL

Greetings! Success begins and ends with God. Start your morning off by first praying to God and thanking Him for another day. Read your *Planting Seeds Devotional*.

The following are some tips to help you be successful in school:

- Write down assignment due dates and test dates as soon as they are announced. Show the assignments to your parents.
- Do your homework or studying right after school.
- Study every day (a little every day, including Saturday and Sunday, equals a lot).
- Always check your assignment twice before turning it in.
- Take your time and take good notes.
- Ask questions.
- Study with someone who is smarter than you.
- Develop a love for reading.
- Eat something before doing your homework or taking a test. This will help your concentration.
- Talk to your parents or guardians about your day. Tell them everything.
- Before going to bed, talk to God and tell Him everything.

Now you're on the road to success. God's blessings to you.

WHAT TO READ WHEN YOU SAY:

❧ I can't	Philippians 4:13
❧ I am worried	Philippians 4:19
❧ I am afraid	II Timothy 1:7
❧ I lack faith	Romans 12:3
❧ I am weak	Psalm 27:1
❧ Satan has taken control	I John 4:4
❧ I feel defeated	II Corinthians 2:14
❧ I lack wisdom	James 1:14
❧ I am depressed	Lamentations 3:21-23
❧ I am upset	I Peter 5:7
❧ I am alone	Matthew 28:20; Hebrews 13:5
❧ I am a failure	Romans 8:37

In times when you are not feeling good,
the only person from whom
you should seek help is God.
The only way to get His advice
is to read His word.
-SND

PURPOSE

- To plant seeds in a generation of children that who will start their days off by reading about God's word.
- To help them plant godly seeds in their minds that they might go out and be a blessing to all around them.

MISSION

- To build a strong relationship between children and God.
- To help children understand just how great God's love is for them that love God.
- To guide and nurture all children.
- To equip children's minds for kingdom building.

VISION

- To compose various writings from various situations in life.
- To relate to children of all races, religious affiliations, and backgrounds.
- To form a sense of oneness between children and God.
- To raise up a generation of children who have known and communicated with God since the start of their grade school years.

WHY YOU SHOULD ORDER YOUR *CHILDREN PLANTING SEEDS FAMILY DAILY DEVOTIONAL*

- To increase your child's awareness of who God is.
- To increase your child's awareness of who he or she is.
- To build self-confidence and self-esteem.
- To enhance your child's reading and vocabulary.

CONCLUSION

I am convinced that what you have read and the assignments that you have completed will help you achieve your dreams. The world is full of unhappy people searching for the right job, car, home, etc., but I know from experience that there is no better feeling than knowing that God has helped you achieve your dreams. The world will offer you many things, but only God will offer you salvation and the desires of your heart. Now take what you have learned and allow it to sink deep into your heart, mind, spirit, and soul. Allow God to lead you over, around, and through the mountains and valleys of this world. Remember that God wants you to be successful. God wants you to be a witness and a blessing to those around you. I promise you that if you start by making a plan and following it as you follow God, all of your dreams will come true.

Now go out into this world prepared to succeed and achieve your dreams.